MY NATIVE LAND A4

Ana Blandiana was born in 1942 in Timişoara, Romania. She has published 14 books of poetry, two of short stories, nine books of essays and one novel. Her work has been translated into 24 languages published in 58 books of poetry and prose to date. In Britain a number of her earlier poems were published in *The Hour of Sand: Selected Poems 1969-1989* (Anvil Press Poetry, 1989), with a later selection in versions by Seamus Heaney in John Fairleigh's contemporary Romanian anthology *When the Tunnels Meet* (Bloodaxe Books, 1996). She was co-founder and President of the Civic Alliance from 1990, an independent non-political organisation that fought for freedom and democratic change. She also re-founded and became President of the Romanian PEN Club, and in 1993, under the aegis of the European Community, she created the Memorial for the Victims of Communism. In recognition of her contribution to European culture and her valiant fight for human rights, Blandiana was awarded the highest distinction of the French Republic, the *Légion d'Honneur* (2009). She has won numerous international literary awards. Her latest book *My Native Land A4* was published in Romania in 2010, and is first published in English by Bloodaxe Books in 2014 (translated by Paul Scott Derrick and Viorica Patea).

ANA BLANDIANA

MY NATIVE LAND A4

TRANSLATED BY

PAUL SCOTT DERRICK
& VIORICA PATEA

BLOODAXE BOOKS

ISBN: 978 1 78037 105 4

First published 2014 by
Bloodaxe Books Ltd,
Eastburn,
South Park,
Hexham,
Northumberland NE46 1BS.

www.bloodaxebooks.com
For further information about Bloodaxe titles
please visit our website or write to
the above address for a catalogue.

Supported by
**ARTS COUNCIL
ENGLAND**

The publication of this book was supported by a grant
from the Romanian Cultural Institute, Bucharest.

INSTITUTUL
CULTURAL
R O M Â N

Cover image: Gabi Marian Photography, facebook.com/gabimarian.ro

Cover design: Neil Astley & Pamela Robertson-Pearce.

Printed in Great Britain by Bell & Bain Limited, Glasgow, Scotland, on
acid-free paper sourced from mills with FSC chain of custody certification.

ACKNOWLEDGEMENTS

My Native Land A4 was first published in Romanian as *Patria Mea A4* by Editura Humanitas, Bucharest, in 2010.

Acknowledgements are due to the editors of the following journals, in which some of the translations from this book have previously appeared: *Liburna: International Journal of Humanities* 5 (November 2012), *Poetry London* 75 (Summer 2013), *Modern Poetry in Translation* 2 (2013), *The Cincinnati Review* 10.2 (Winter 2014) and *The Literary Review* 5.05 (Winter 2014).

The afterword, 'Poetry Between Silence and Sin', was written by Ana Blandiana as a synthesis of her poetics for a lecture she delivered at the invitation of La Cattedra di Poesia of Il Centro Internazionale Eugenio Montale in Rome in 1999.

The translators would also like to express their gratitude to John Fairleigh for his very helpful advice and to Ana Blandiana for her extreme generosity and kindness.

CONTENTS

Ana Blandiana: The Country Beyond the Country

Anna Akhmatova's most important book of poems, *Requiem*, describes the suffering of the Russian people under Stalinism. In a prefatory note, entitled 'Instead of a Preface', the poet recalls:

> [...] I spent seventeen months in the prison queues in Leningrad. One day someone 'identified' me. Then a woman with lips blue with cold who was standing behind me, and of course had never heard of my name, came out of the numbness which affected us all and whispered in my ear – (we all spoke only in whispers then):
> 'Could you describe this?'
> I said, 'I can!'
> Then something resembling a smile slipped over what had once been her face.[1]

Akhmatova composed, memorised and reworked this elegy in secret during the years of Stalin's great terror (1935-1940), and dared write it down only in 1957. The book was published six years later in Munich and appeared posthumously in the USSR in 1987. *Requiem* was written in response to the imprisonment of her son – she had lost two husbands and many friends executed or exiled in prison camps – a period during which she stood in queues outside jails waiting for news or a chance to send a small package or a message to him, or other relatives and friends. The poem bears witness to the tribulations of other women in similar situations, to their sense of grief and powerlessness, as well as to common suffering and shared community. In her prefatory note, Akhmatova defines the role of the poet as a witness of history and defends the potential of poetry to defeat injustice, suffering, and arbitrary power. It is the poet's duty to bear witness to the experience of those victims whose suffering would otherwise remain ignored, muted, unknown.

---

1. Anna Akhmatova, *Selected Poems*, tr. Richard McKane (Newcastle upon Tyne: Bloodaxe Books, 1989), 281.

The place that Ana Blandiana, the pen name of Otilia Valeria Coman (*b.* Timişoara, 1942), occupies in the literary life of Romania is comparable to that of Anna Akhmatova in Russia or Václav Havel in the Czech Republic. A highly acclaimed figure of Romanian letters, she has written fourteen books of poetry, two books of fantastic prose, seven books of essays, and one novel. Her work has been translated into twenty-six languages and grouped into forty-seven books of poetry and prose to date. Blandiana can be placed among those poets who conceive literature as a form of resistance against what Mircea Eliade refers to as the 'terror of history'.

Havel viewed the writer's mission as 'the duty to tell the truth about the world in which he lives, to speak of its horrors and miseries' so that 'the slogans and fanaticism of abstraction shouldn't replace respect for the individual'.[2] In the same way, Blandiana affirms her determination 'to hold on to those values which the system has attempted to destroy in order to prevail'. In her view, 'we exist only to the degree that we make ourselves witnesses to history, a history which, in turn, only exists to the degree that we witness it'.[3] Like Havel, Akhmatova, Ivan Chmeliov, or Solzhenitsyn, Blandiana is aware that bearing witness is a legacy that the writer passes on to future generations.

Blandiana was a prominent opponent of the Ceauşescu regime, and her daring, outspoken poems, along with her courageous attitude in the defence of ethical values, made her a legendary figure in Romanian literature. Many critics have compared her with other iconic figures and called her a new Joan of Arc, a mythic Hecuba or Cassandra grieving for the fate of her people among the ruins of the present. Over the years, her works have become symbols of an ethical consciousness that refuses to be silenced by a totalitarian government. Blandiana believes that writers serve as witnesses of their time and that literature is a form of moral resistance to the

---

2. Václav Havel, *Interrogatoire à distance* (Paris: Éditions de l'Aube, 1989), 13; and *Essais politiques* (Paris: Calmann-Levy, 1990), 233.

3. Ana Blandiana, *Spaima de literatură* (Bucharest: Humanitas, 2004), 106, 32.

hardships of history. In the murky political panorama after 1989, she became an image of hope. Her idealistic assertions embodied the faith of all those who embraced democratic values and believed that 'living in truth', in Havel's formulation, was an imperative. And her exemplary life has authenticated the ideals she strove for. She represents the archetype of the writer whose work and life have become emblematic of a collective destiny. Blandiana's work is symbolic of a conscience that cannot be subdued by any totalitarian regime. Her stance, like that of the Spanish existentialist philosopher Miguel de Unamuno, defies those who exercise the 'reason of force' by countering with 'the force of reason'.

* * *

Blandiana was born in Timişoara, the city that would later become the birthplace of the 1989 Revolution, to Gheorghe Coman, a graduate in law and theology, a high-school teacher and a charismatic Orthodox priest, and to Otilia Diacu, an accountant who raised her two daughters alone during her husband's long years of detention.

Her literary debut at the age of 17, with a poem entitled 'Originality' published in the Transylvanian journal *Tribuna*, brought about the first of a series of prohibitions of her work. In 1906, at her father's request, Anna Andreyevna Gorenko took the pen name Akhmatova to spare her family the dishonour of her 'decadent' poems. Half a century later, at exactly the same age, Otilia Valeriu Coman chose a pseudonym in order to hide her true identity from the secret police, since her father was, at that time, in and out of jail as a political prisoner. However, the Communist authorities soon discovered her true identity and declared her the daughter of 'an enemy of the people', and a nationwide ban was issued forbidding all journals and publishing houses to print her poems. For four years she was denied the right to publish or to pursue her university studies. This aborted literary debut was followed by three more bans on her writing (1959-64, 1985, 1988-89). She suffered reprisals and prohibitions under two Communist dictatorships, those of Gheorghe Gheorghiu-Dej (1947-64), during her adolescence, and Nicolae Ceauşescu (1965-89).

Her pen name, Ana Blandiana, bears the aura of magic and carries mythological associations. Blandiana is the name of her mother's picturesque village on the banks of the river Mureş in Transylvania; and Ana, which she chose for its rhyme, is also the name of the heroine of 'The Artist Manole', a traditional Romanian ballad which illustrates the idea that sacrifice lies at the foundation of all creation. In the ballad, Manole, the master builder in charge of the construction of the most beautiful monastery, is told in a dream that the curse which made the sanctuary fall down every night can be dispelled only if someone who is very dear to him or to his masons is immured in it. They agree that the victim should be the first woman who comes at dawn to bring them food. And this turns out to be Ana, Manole's wife, whom he walls in only to commit suicide afterwards. Blandiana assumed something like the heroine's sacrificial destiny during the gloomy decades of dictatorship. Later she became aware that her pseudonym represented a mysterious legacy she had to bear out in time.[4] And Ana – a name charged with so many mythical associations – became the very expression of her being. In 'Ballad', a poem written before 1989, she avows:

> I have no other Ana.
> I wall myself up in myself
> But who can tell if it's enough?
> The wall doesn't fall on its own.
> It's being torn down by a whimsical bulldozer
> Aimlessly walking through a nightmare
> In its sleep.
>
> [...]
>
> I have no other Ana.
> In fact, I even have
> Less and less of myself.

In 1960, Blandiana married the writer, historian and film critic, Romulus Rusan, when she was 18. She graduated in Romance

---

4. Ana Blandiana, *Spaima de literatură*, 155.

philology and literature at the University of Cluj. Her second and irrevocable debut was in 1964 with the publication of *First Person Plural*, a premonitory title that announced her deep concern with the 'other', despite the fact that the poems of this collection celebrate the exuberance of the senses. In 1967 the couple moved to Bucharest where Blandiana worked as a librarian at the Institute of Fine Arts, as well as an editor at the literary journals *Viaţa studentească* and *Amfiteatru*, where she would later publish her incendiary poems of protest. From 1974 to 1988 she contributed regularly to *România literară*.

Blandiana belongs to the Generation of the Sixties, a group of young poets born in 1940s, such as Nichita Stănescu, Marin Sorescu, Ioan Alexandru, and Ileana Malăncioiu, as well as some poets from older generations, like Stefan Augustin Doinaş, whose works had been forbidden during the 1950s. Taking advantage of a spell of political liberalisation, the poets of this somewhat heterogeneous movement, also called the 'Neo-Modernists', had one common aspiration: to reestablish the dialogue, interrupted by decades of enforced indoctrination of socialist realism or *proletcult*, with the poets of the 20s and 30s, such as George Bacovia, Lucian Blaga, Tudor Arghezi and Ion Barbu. In defiance of the official ideology, the Neo-Modernists adopted a metaphoric and hermetic language and embraced an aesthetic idiom which, by its mere aestheticism, subverted the official ideological indoctrination. Aspiring towards 'pure poetry', these poets engaged in introspection and philosophical meditations with strong metaphysical accents.

Over the years, Blandiana wrote a series of poetry collections – *Achilles' Heel* (1966), *The Third Sacrament* (1969), *October, November, December* (1972), *The Sleep within Sleep* (1977), *The Cricket's Eye* (1981) and *The Predator Star* (1985) – which established her as one of the most prominent poets of her generation. She soon established herself as a prolific, highly lauded, multi-prizewinning poet, celebrated by the Romanian Academy and the Writers' Union. In 1982, she became the youngest recipient of the Gottfried von Herder Prize. The Austrian Academy's recognition of her work highlighted 'the supra-temporal dimension that themes like purity and sin, death and survival, love as aspiration for the absolute and escape from materiality, confer to her poetry'. The jury declared that the prize had been awarded in 'appreciation of her poetic and essayistic work, which represents a profound meditation on artistic creation and the human being, and which consecrates poetry as a creating myth without falling into the trap of facile biography and artificiality'.

The international recognition and prestige she won forced the Communist authorities to allow the publication of her highly subversive collection of fantastic prose, *Projects of the Past* (1982), the sequel to *The Four Seasons* (1977), which at the time was being censured for its 'anti-social tendencies'. *Projects of the Past*, a fresco of recent Romanian history beginning with the establishment of the Communist régime, was to become Blandiana's most frequently translated book. Her short stories follow the tradition of Poe, E.T.A. Hoffmann and Kafka, and are reminiscent of the fantastic prose of Mikhail Bulgakov's *The Master and Margarita*, or the magical realism of Latin American writers such as Jorge Luis Borges and Julio Cortázar.

Journalistic and poetic, these stories, written in first person, combine incursions of visionary imagination with confessional autobiography and the realistic evocation of documentary prose. More than fiction, they seem to represent a diary in which meditation and lucidity acquire the intensity of a revelatory dream. At the same time, Blandiana makes an important contribution to the theories of the fantastic formulated by Pierre-Georges Castex, Roger Caillois, Louis Vax, Tzvetan Todorov, Jorge Luis Borges and Julio Cortázar. In her view, 'the fantastic is not opposed to the real, but is instead its deepest and most meaningful representation since, after all, to imagine means to remember'.[5] For her, the fantastic is not premised on a split between two different worlds, but on their continuity and unity. In Blandiana's prose and poems the fantastic is, in the words of one critic, 'enamoured of the real'.[6]

---

5. *Spaima de literatură*, 118.
6. Valeriu Cristea, 'Fantasticul îndrăgostit de real', *România Literară*, XVI: 1, 6 January 1983, 4; Iulian Boldea, *Ana Blandiana* (Braşov: Editura Aula, 2000).

In late December of 1984 Blandiana managed to circumvent the draconian censorship of the government and published a series of four poems – 'The Children's Crusade', 'I Believe', 'Delimitations' and 'Everything' – in the avant-garde journal *Amfiteatru*. The distribution of the journal was cancelled, but handwritten copies of these poems continued to circulate underground. They were, in fact, the first *samizdat* poems in Romanian literature, denouncing a political system that constantly falsified reality and destroyed human dignity. The content of her poems got Blandiana into serious trouble, so much so that she feared for her life. Reprisals against her were harsh, but she was helped by international solidarity and the backing of Italian and German intellectuals. In the UK, *The Independent* gave full coverage to this incident, publishing the series of poems and glossing 'Everything' line by line, so that Western readers could appreciate its subversive reading of daily life in Romania.[7]

In 1988, after a temporary easing of the political grip, Blandiana published a poem for children, 'Motanul Arpagic' ('Tomcat Onion'), a thinly disguised satire of Ceauşescu, represented by an arrogant Tomcat who seizes the street and behaves as if he owns the entire world. This poem brought her tremendous notoriety, and was predictably followed by a new ban. Reprisals against her were fierce. The poet's name was erased from any public reference and her books were removed from libraries. Under heavy surveillance by the secret police, she became a virtual prisoner in her own home: a car was parked in front of her house, visitors were intimidated, postal correspondence was controlled, the telephone cut off, and her outings hindered. This situation lasted until Ceauşescu's downfall in December 1989, when Blandiana was elected, without her knowledge, to the newly formed National Salvation Front. A month later she resigned, having realised that former dissidents were being manipulated for propagandist purposes by a neo-Communist government.

---

7. Kevin Jackson, 'Underground Notes', *The Independent*, Saturday 18 February 1989.

The poems she wrote during the second half of the 80s were published after the revolution in *The Architecture of Waves* (1990). She also published a highly sophisticated postmodern novel in 1992, *The Drawer Full of Applause*, about the destiny of an author who is writing a book he knows will never be published while struggling against the persecution and surveillance of the secret police. Since then she has produced five more books of poetry: *One Hundred Poems* (1991), *Harvest of Angels* (1997), *The Sun of the Hereafter* (2000), *The Ebb of the Senses* (2004), and *My Native Land: A4* (2010); and a celebrated collection of essays, *The Anxiety of Literature* (2006), on the meaning of literature and the writer's role in the contemporary world.

Deeply believing that moral values should be translated into political reality, Blandiana was active in the civil rights movement in defence of democratic values. She became an important public figure as a co-founder and President of the 'Civic Alliance' (1990-2001), an independent non-political organisation that fought for freedom and democratic change. Yet Blandiana systematically rejected numerous political positions offered to her by various political parties wanting to take advantage of her popularity and moral credit, from presidential to ministerial portfolios to diplomatic and well-remunerated appointments in international organisations. Although it would have been very profitable to become a dignitary in the political arena, she preferred to claim only one title: that of poet, thus reviving the ideal figure of the artist who remains immune from cynical games of power.

It would be a mistake to call Blandiana's work political, despite the fact that it contains political statements. Her notion of politics is similar to that of the ancient Greeks, who conceived political involve-ment as a civic responsibility of every individual vis à vis the *polis*. Just as she took it upon herself to denounce the human rights violations of Ceauşescu's dictatorship, so after 1989 she saw it as her duty to condemn the manipulation of democratic values by the new political power. And despite her intense civic activity and participation in protest marches and meetings, she devoted herself with an almost mystical asceticism to writing and to the memory of the victims.

In 1990 Blandiana re-founded the Romanian PEN Club (founded in 1924 and dissolved during the Communist period) and assumed its Presidency. This was the first institution to re-establish Romania's position in the Western world. Under the aegis of the European Council, Blandiana and her husband have recently founded the 'Memorial for the Victims of Communism' located in Sighet in the northern part of Romania. A research centre for historical studies, it is considered the third most important museum of the European conscience after Auschwitz and the Normandy memorial. The motto of the Memorial is Blandiana's phrase 'if justice does not succeed in being a form of memory, memory alone can be a form of justice'. The Memorial is based on the conviction that democracy will always be menaced by ignorance of the true nature of any totalitarian regime and its ambition to create a 'new man'. In recognition of her contribution to European culture and her valiant fight for human rights, in 2009 Blandiana was awarded the highest distinction of the French Republic, the *Légion d'Honneur*.

Blandiana redefines her poetics in every new book of poetry she publishes. *My Native Land A4*, the fourth collection written since 1989, springs from an awareness that the poet's identity is grounded in writing. Poetic creation is Blandiana's ultimate form of self-definition and the boundaries set out by her writing circumscribe her homeland, the only homeland the poet can finally belong to. In this volume she projects visionary spaces within the confines of a page – A4 in Europe, similar to US Letter – as anguished territories in which the lyrical 'I' is compelled to try to draw precise, clear boundaries out of a diffuse magma of words.

Her poems articulate a quest for love, beauty and truth and affirm an urgent need for existential authenticity as a requisite for the redemption of the self. Reduced to the condition of 'broken balloons' (in 'He'), or that of 'empty forms [...] squeezed dry/ Of the honey of eternity' (in 'Honeycombs'), Blandiana's poetic persona hovers 'between this shadowy room of the flesh' and 'the light of afterwards' (in 'Like a Rubber Band'). Her poetry chronicles the struggle between a constantly deteriorating body that is learning how to die and the spirit that strives to overcome its physical constraints.

My Native Land A4 includes meditations on fundamental themes, such as the fragility and vulnerability of being, the inexorable toll of time, the limitations of the human condition and the correspondence between life and death within the cosmic rhythms of the universe. This stateless no-man's land of the blank page, home of a poet who feels herself to be an exile in the present world, is inhabited by fallen angels, burning seraphim or a flock of pigeons 'sitting in obedient pairs/ On the sloping roof of the church' symbolising the poems themselves or the white pages of a book, 'too many/ Clones of the Holy Ghost' ('Pigeons'), indistinguishable among so many simulacra.

As in her earlier work, in which she strove to achieve 'clear tones and colours' ('The Gift'),[8] in this collection she continues to aspire towards purity and adopts an ethical stance which, given the general spiritual bankruptcy of modern civilisation, condemns her to solitude, to a 'loneliness [that] takes the form of crowds' while 'crowds become deserts' ('The Strap of the Rucksack'). This yearning for purity is menaced by the ceaseless thrust of the quotidian, which brings about degradation and chaos. Thus, in 'Above the River', art is compared to an icon hung above a bridge, symbolising the arch of eternity presiding over time's incessant flow towards death.

'The great law of maculation', Blandiana confesses in an earlier poem, is the tribute we pay in order to live, since 'purity does not bear fruit' and 'virgins do not bear children' ('I Know Purity'). Just as Midas changes everything he touches into gold, the poet's fate is to transform everything 'into words' ('The Gift'). For her, poetry arouses both the wonder of contemplation and the happiness of despair. That is, she takes great joy in her gift, but she also sees it as an implacable temptation that takes possession of her. Blandiana writes with the sense that she is trapped in a shifting field of impersonal, unknown forces, as for example, in 'Hunt in Time'. She writes from

---

8. Ana Blandiana, *Poeme 1964-2004* (Bucharest: Humanitas, 2008).

the solitude of someone confined by the virtual condition of speech, caught in the changing web of significations of her own meanings, entombed, as she says in 'Amber', in 'this luminous crypt of words'.

After years of engaging in solitary moral debates, her poems at times express a form of ritualised suffering. Blandiana identifies with the pain of others and assumes it as her own: 'I've privatised the pain/ And now, all around me/ It's closed up in the walls of my flesh,/ Like a magnet that has pulled it in from the world.' ('Beyond this Body'). The lyrical 'I' feels responsible for the vulnerability of the world and, as a consequence, that implacable 'law of maculation' becomes a foundational obsession.

Blandiana takes on the role of an impartial witness who, as though from the corner of a painting, meditates on modern man's increasing superficiality in a world with no vertical projection. She is an impotent observer of the inexorable process of negative becoming; a process that brings about the loss of primordial meanings in a world in which spiritual paradigms have been replaced by power games and consumer values. From the vantage point of a street 'going downhill' on a 'slope' that 'is getting more and more dangerous' ('The Slope'), she casts an eye on the desolate panorama of the contemporary world, which has lost the notion of the transcendent and seems to be confined within the parameters of avarice and hate.

Many of Blandiana's poems affirm a deep ecological concern for the fragility of nature, a deep respect for 'the other', whether animal, tree or rock. Ecological consciousness is an older theme of her poems, which raises the more general question of how guilty we are when we passively watch the massacre of the innocent. 'Animal Planet', a poem which takes its title from the popular documentary channel, evokes the image of 'the placid and ferocious lion as it tears a fawn to pieces'. This incident serves as a larger metaphor of our responsibility towards life. 'The laws of nature' which 'decide/ Who should kill whom/ And whoever kills most is king' are also the laws that rule our human world. The refusal to watch or to acknowledge the continuing massacres does not exonerate us from responsibility for these atrocities. Violent consumer entertainment is part of a daily routine in which forms of religious consolation are no longer readily available:

> Less guilty, though not innocent,
> In any case more innocent than you,
> The author of this pitiless perfection,
> Who set up this design
> And afterward, taught me to turn the other cheek.

('Animal Planet')

The modern world is a world from which God appears to be absent. Engrossed by the dynamics of market consumerism, modern men 'buy and sell, buy and sell,' and 'eat on the run'. They traverse their own lives blind to the spiritual dimension of existence. They move through 'the shadows of reality −/ Shadows they believe to be real' ('Closed Churches'). High up in the mountains, 'the strap of the rucksack' rubs against the stumps of feathers of what had once been wings on our backs. Below, under a flat horizon, 'Harried citizens' 'trundle by on roller skates', bent on mechanical pilgrimages. Blind and deaf to the world that surrounds them, and conveniently insulated by their mobile phone conversations, they cannot read the signs of nature announcing the passage of time and their own finitude:

> And their eyes glued to monitors,
> Unaware that the leaves are falling now
> And the birds are flying away.
> They trundle by on roller skates
> While the seasons roll over in the whispering air above them.
> Lives,
> Years, centuries,
> And they never understand.'

('On Roller Skates')

In the age of progress, generation has been reconceived as the proliferation of a series of mechanisms. Blandiana alters the Biblical definition of man who finds his identity in the image of God to men conceived as 'Mechanical devices/ Created by other mechanical devices/ In their image and likeness.' These techno-adolescents are finally aided by a compassionate God who descends and 'learns to roller skate/ In order to save them.' ('On Roller Skates').

A new theme in Blandiana's more recent poetry is her reproach to God for the unjust way he made the world. Her God is the 'author of a pitiless perfection' ('Animal Planet') and the 'God of guilt' who has decided on his own 'the ratio of good and evil' ('Prayer'). In one of the most surprising poems of the collection, she addresses the 'God of the dragonflies, of nocturnal moths,/ Of larks and owls,/ God of earthworms and scorpions,/ Of kitchen cockroaches' and wonders on what grounds he 'settled/ On the sizes/ Of their poisons, colours and perfumes', and what made him decide to place 'a song in one beak/ And a cackle in another,/ Murder in one soul and ecstasy in another'. The poem is entitled 'Prayer', yet it proves to be a lengthy indictment of God for creating – or at least allowing – the injustice of the world. This is an imperfect and arbitrary God, reminiscent of Emil Cioran's 'bad demiurge', who does not come close to the goodness of his son:

> The scales trembling always in a delicate balance
> Above the wounded body
> Of your son, who
> Does not resemble you at all.

Nevertheless, in spite of such a desolate panorama, Blandiana affirms the existence of spiritual values and her poetic universe is open to hope. The city may be the space of unease, from which the sacred has been expelled, but nature is suffused with mystery and can provide salvation. In 'Out in the Hills', for example, the lyric persona lies back in a meadow beneath the sky, engages in communion with the soul, earth and heavens and recovers her purified self: 'Lying on my back in the high meadow [...] My soul/ Gets used to the earth/ And takes a deep breath'.

This kind of Whitmanesque 'loafing' is also suggested in 'Exorcism'. There, walking 'barefoot on the grass', she sheds her socially

constructed identity and is possessed (or possibly re-possessed) by a
spirit that rises up through her soles from the earth:

> I give myself completely to the grass.
> It soothes
> My uneasiness –
> And I leave only the naked soles of my feet in the dew,
> Through which you ascend
> To inhabit me.

Blandiana's paradoxical and allegorical language dwells on the
frontier between two different orders of being, the concrete physical
reality of the here and now and a time beyond time, 'that painful
dawn/ From the other side' ('The Hidden Light'). Sometimes, as in
'Eardrum', her words actually become 'That border [...] Stretched
between two worlds/ Like an eardrum' whose only function is to
'transmit in vain [...] The nothing/ That can not become a syllable'.
Or, as in 'Hollow Walls', the poetic persona is aware that she inhabits
a liminal space: 'We are here/ Between hollow walls [...]. And we
feel good [...] In this world/ From which we learn to die.'

And death, or that patient but unrelenting need to learn how to
die, is the central motif of this book. Its core poem, and arguably
the most moving one, was composed as an elegy for Blandiana's
mother. But 'Requiem' expands the conventions of the elegy and
changes it into a mournful affirmation of the transcendence of being.
Bedridden with cancer and suffering a terrible pain that even
morphine will not soften, the poet's mother prays to God to put an
end to her life. And, while an angel watches with tensed wings from
the head of the bed to see if she is still breathing, mother and daughter
carry out a dialogue ripe with implicit meaning in the face of an
outcome they are both fully aware of:

> I said to you
> 'A poet, whom I don't think you've read,
> Believed that
> In the beyond

There is also death
And its outcome is to be born on the earth.'
And, for a moment, you forgot your pain,
You smiled at me,
Sad,
As though it were a joke,
And I went on, to make you laugh:
'If you don't feel at home there,
Remember Novalis.
And, above all, don't forget
To tie a knot in your handkerchief
To let me know
When you're coming back.'

A voice from childhood tells her 'There is here' and the limit between the two worlds, between life and death, time and eternity disappears. Both realms are integrated into a new whole in which life is not lost but transfigured. In this worldview, whether we consider it religious or philosophical, death is not a conclusion, but a passage to another condition of being. 'Requiem' captures this very moment of passage, of matter dissolving into light, in which the antinomies of time, matter and spirit are reconciled in a higher unity:

You were so lovely,
Almost translucent –
Still a body, but a body
That contained a light that
Drew your shape on the pillow,
A silver-tinted shadow –
Even then, a shadow
You began to belong
To another world, to another state of being
Even then,
Even before.

Blandiana's deceptively simple language expresses itself in homely images, parables and metaphors in the tradition of the Metaphysical poets or Emily Dickinson. Her poems begin with the concrete, and often the ordinary – the description of trees, the light of a candle, leaves changing colour in autumn, doves, the flow of a river, amber – and lead to the realm of the spiritual. These commonplace things become metaphors of emotional states or philosophical and existential concepts. As Allen Tate so famously said of Dickinson, 'she does not separate [abstractions] from the sensuous illuminations that she is so marvellously adept at; like Donne, she perceives abstraction and thinks sensation'.[9] It would be safe to say that Blandiana concurs with T.S. Eliot's Modernist agenda in favour of a poetic language based on a 'direct sensuous apprehension of thought, or a recreation of thought into feeling'.[10]

With its constant play between light and darkness, the foreseeable and the unexpected, and drawing on a profound ethical subtext, Blandiana's poetry presents a variety of meanings. The hallmark of her lyric is an aphoristic and philosophical language that oscillates between the sacred and the profane. Her poetics exploits the power of suggestion, presents an architecture of silence, and engages in a constant tension between what is said and what is left unsaid.

Blandiana's voice is lucid and free of easy sentimentality. Her poetic discourse is characterised by restraint and a graceful control of inner turmoil. Like many of the Anglo-American Modernists, Ana Blandiana believes that poetry is above all suggestion, the art of saying much (of saying more than you've said) with the fewest and least pretentious words you can manage to find.

VIORICA PATEA
PAUL SCOTT DERRICK

---

9. Allen Tate, *Reactionary Essays on Poetry and Ideas* (New York: Charles Scribner's Sons, 1936), 13.

10. T. S. Eliot, 'Shakespeare and the Stoicism of Seneca' in *Selected Essays* (London: Faber and Faber, 1972), 286.

MY NATIVE LAND A4

In the Frescoes

In their hands, the founders carry
Heavy monasteries,
Like expendable capital
In the exchange office of the afterlife.
Young monks
With PhDs from Cambridge
And ageing peasant women
Venerate liturgical ornaments
And crawl on their knees
Across flagstones with Cyrillic inscriptions:
Loudspeakers
Transmit the mass
As far as the yard, crowded with tents,
As far as the roadside where
Parked cars
Are waiting to be blessed;
While faith –
Like the swallows
That circle and dart inside the cupola
Frightened by the bells –
Reels in fear,
Crashes into the painted walls
Of the Pantocrator,
Descends,
And obediently alights in the frescoes.

How Hard It Is to Caress

How hard it is to caress the feathers of an angel!
No matter how close, it flees from your touch,
Afraid that you might trap it,
Flies around in circles, and then comes back –
The noiseless flutter of its wings
Is the only sound it can produce.
Angels don't know how to talk,
Words are not fine enough
To express them.
Their muted message is their presence.
At times they come up close
To surround you with their aura
But then they dart away, frightened by the intimacy.
Protective, but not familiar,
They always keep a distance across which
My words are straining to get to them.
I can never know if these words are not too weak for them to hear.
The handicap of faith!
Not to know if they hear you; not to know if you hear.
Of all the senses, only the dream of touch remains,
The dream, without scaring it, of touching the feathers of an angel…

Animal Planet

Less guilty, though not innocent,
In this universe where
The laws of nature decide
Who should kill whom
And whoever kills most is king.
How admiringly they film
The placid and ferocious lion as it tears a fawn to pieces!
And whenever I close my eyes or switch off the telly,
I feel that I participate less in the crime,
Even though the candle of life
Will always need blood to go on burning –
The blood of another.

Less guilty, though not innocent,
I sat at table with the hunters,
Nevertheless, I loved to caress the long and silky
Ears of hares
Lying in stacks, like a tumulus
On top of an embroidered tablecloth.
Guilty, even though I didn't
Pull the trigger,
And I covered my ears
Horrified by the sound of death
And by the smell of the shameless sweat of the hunters who fired
          the shots.

Less guilty, though not innocent,
In any case more innocent than you,
The author of this pitiless perfection,
Who set up this design
And afterwards, taught me to turn the other cheek.

Hourglass

I contemplate the hourglass
Where a grain of sand
Got stuck
And refuses to fall.
It's like a dream:
Nothing moves.
I contemplate the mirror:
Nothing changes.
A dream of stopping
On the road towards death
Is the same as being dead.

Carnival

He covers himself in motley
And passes from leaf to leaf
In his brilliant disguise, gently
To convince them that flying does no harm,
That the freedom will make them thrive.
And then he lets them go.
Set loose for the very first time in their lives,
They find the experience charms,
As though they were never going to die.
But then, they do.
And he, who dressed them up
To take their lives away,
Is left there alone, covered all in motley,
Like a clown
In a world that's suddenly grown
Too big,
Between the cathedral and the square,
Alone, unable to die
Even though he knows how to fly.

The Owner of the Mill

What is it made of,
That dust that he leaves over things,
So fine (it's almost invisible)
It only duplicates their contours with a halo of shadow?
Where is the mill that grinds down everything that disappears
And produces this sawdust of non-being?
Like a powder that sticks to your fingers
When you want to caress something out of the past.
Or maybe he's the one who's been ground up,
So that no one will notice when he disappears
And no one will remember
The difference between
The finite cold
And burning eternity.
But in that case, who is the owner of that mill where
Death is nothing but a pale manipulation?

The Tale of the Calendar

I wasn't yet,
Only you knew that I was going to be.
And in spite of that, you set the Annunciation
Without consulting me.
Or maybe no one consulted you either?
Were you also faced
With predetermined facts?
In any case, what could I have decided
While I was swimming in amniotic fluid,
Loving
The covering of ardent flesh
That was about to undress me
And throw me naked
Into the world
Wrapped in the placenta – just as in a tale…
Tell me the truth: were you afraid of me?
Of how I grew inside of you
Threatening to replace you?
Was it out of fear that you decided
To place between us
The tale of the calendar?

Hunt in Time

I feel that I'm the prey,
But I don't know whose,
Since the wings and claws that hover
Above me,
And chain me to the shadow
Long before they reach me,
Have no name.
Only a breath of cooler air suggests
The slow approach
Of that crude and voluptuous threat.

I know there's no salvation, but
I don't know what salvation would be.
If I try to run away, the shadow also changes,
Moulding itself to my horizon like the clouds,
Ferocious and protective, so careful
Not to lose me, to let me fall prey to another.

While I wait, the thrills become confused
And terror mixes pleasantly into the mystery
Whose unravelling will be my fate.
I have to live until I find the answer –
Exactly as long as this hunt
In which, at least, I know that I'm the prey.

Agglomeration

They could never be sure that spring would come back.
Buried under mountains of snow,
They didn't know whether the sun would melt them.
And every year they waited, impatient,
For the buds to open again.

What an exciting life! What tumultuous emotions,
When even the smallest event was shepherded by a god
That had to be prayed to, begged and adored –
A god that extorted sacrifices – i.e., metaphysical bribes –
In order to carry out his appointed duties.

And the little gods, for their part, depended on bigger gods,
And the good gods were opposed by other vengeful gods,
And every square inch of ground was inhabited
By endless hierarchies of invisible beings.
How marvellous to walk around among them
And not to bother anyone.

Closed Churches

Closed churches
Like houses whose owners have gone away
Without saying when they'll be back
And without any forwarding address.
Bicycles and trams run all
Around the city.
Claxons, shouts,
The harried citizens
Buy and sell, buy and sell,
They eat on the run
And every now and then
They stop for a coffee
At a pavement café
Near an eleventh-century cathedral
That they look at and never see
Since they're talking into a phone
And never even think to ask
Who it was that lived there,
One day, long ago,
In such an opulent house.

Out in the Hills

Out in the hills, your soul
Can catch its breath,
The green there does it good.
It wallows in the early grass,
Half herb, half aroma,
It takes a deep breath, in…out,
Spring opens up inside
And dissipates all of its fear.

Lying on my back in the high meadow,
I watch the clouds as they glide across the sky
Like the smell of hay flowing over the hills,
My eyes and nose
Discover the mystery:
This sweet, tireless spinning in the chaos
That whirls around the spindle of the breathing air,
Aromas and clouds.

And all the while
My soul
Gets used to the earth
And takes a deep breath.

As Though in a Mirror

Before the close of the day
The sun, going down, turns redder
And the moon, coming up, is red.
They're almost the same.

The grass, parched by the heat,
And the stiff teeth of the rake
Like a beard of days –
Place them side by side and
The blackened lines on their faces
Are almost the same.

This soft confusion
Like the moment when you leave
And you turn around for one last look
And you see yourself, as though in a mirror
Being born.

Exorcism

When I walk barefoot on the grass
Electricity flows through me
And down into the earth
Just as the devil,
Forced to leave
The body of the possessed,
Goes down into the earth
At the order of the exorcist.

I give myself completely to the grass.
It soothes
My uneasiness –
And I leave only the naked soles of my feet in the dew,
Through which you ascend
To inhabit me.

Atmosphere

The horizons wrap tightly around me
Like bandages
To heal my wounds,
To stop the bleeding.
Beyond them, layers of discord, dark uncertain mists,
Swirl around everything, just the way the atmosphere swirls
Around the earth.

Crowds come close,
Curious, they touch my wounds,
Infect them,
Filling every orifice,
Ear, nose, mouth,
Every crevice with hate –
I'm deaf, I'm dumb, I'm strangled,
Exhausted, freedom gradually gives way:
Nature hates a vacuum.

On Roller Skates

They trundle by on roller skates
With earphones droning in their ears
And their eyes glued to monitors,
Unaware that the leaves are falling now
And the birds are flying away.
They trundle by on roller skates
While the seasons roll over in the whispering air above them.
Lives,
Years, centuries,
And they never understand.
They trundle by on roller skates,
Darting among the shadows of reality –
Shadows they believe to be real
And characters they think are men,
Mechanical devices
Created by other mechanical devices
In their image and likeness
While God
Comes down
And learns to roller skate
In order to save them.

Heads or Tails

Like the hardly decipherable
Face of a coin tossed up in the air,
Ready to fall and decide
   – Heads or tails –
Not knowing what fate it will seal:
That's how I saw you
As you fell
Across the sky,
Tearing the clouds into strands of white
That wrapped you like a shroud,
As though you already knew
That you'd land at the end
On the asphalt where I waited
To read my fate
In the entrails of an angel.

Honeycombs

You haven't been born
But you're born
Every moment,
And you do not try
To be there, when you're here,
Or here when you go there.
You are that substance audaciously saved
Between one breath and another,
Without which we wouldn't exist.
In the end, we are nothing more
Than remains, empty forms,
Honeycombs, squeezed dry
Of the honey of eternity.

Like a Rubber Band

The moment between the lightning's flash
And its deafening roar,
As tense as a rubber band
About to break,
Burning,
Ties me here
To the rack,
Between this shadowy room of the flesh
And the light of afterwards.

This solemn fear:
I can't go forward
I can't go back.

Season's End

Wrinkles cover the vault,
Like ageing skin
Too big for what it tries to hide:
That abyss
From which the gods were banished
Is smaller now.
A temporary air, provisional,
An air of season's end
Fills the universe
With dust forgotten in the corners
And empty warehouses
Where meaningless poems are declaimed.

Star signs change:
Stupidity, suicidal,
Takes over
Unaware.

The Strap of the Rucksack

The view from this mountaintop:
Fir trees buffeted by raging winds,
Dark, humid valleys, almost obscene,
And other mountaintops, smaller and larger,
Watchful, measuring each other up.

Deciduous populations submit to the seasons
With a wisdom the rains wear away
And insatiable vermin hide
Among the tangled branches.

What serenity in the face of a million defeats!

Loneliness takes the form of crowds
And crowds become deserts.
This retreat to the mountaintops beneath the weight
Of hesychastic silences is growing less secure.
On the edges of shoulder-blades
The strap of the rucksack
Rubs against the stumps of feathers.

Amber

I forget the world, and myself. Slowly
Loneliness fills me up – like mead
That flows into an empty cup
And satisfies its need.

Sacred honeycombs make it, to submerge
My remains under layers of gold
When your limpid punishment, Demiurge,
Wraps me in the delicious mould.

No calvary, but a voluptuous hell
Where I recall my living self, preserved
Like a dragonfly trapped in an amber cell –
This luminous crypt of words.

Biography

When I was a child I noticed how the leaves
Would tremble in step with my thought.
And when I walked away, the stems of plants
Bending almost free of the earth, tried to follow me.

Afterwards, flocks and flocks of birds
Began to fly all around me;
They stopped their songs to listen to mine.
Only when savage beasts also began
To follow my steps, obedient,
I panicked. But then it was too late.

Now I have no right to stop.
Every unspoken poem, every undiscovered word
Puts the universe, suspended
On my lips, at risk.
A single caesura in the line
Would end this magic that dissolves the laws of hate
And throw them all – the lonely and the wild –
Back into the swampy pit of the instincts.

On Tiptoe

I have tiptoed
Up to the line,
I only wanted to touch it
    With the tip of my naked foot,
Like in summer, when I caress the line
    Between the land and the sea.
But the boundary drew back
As though it wanted to protect itself from me –
I keep going forward
Over this sand moistened by death,
Alive and proud
That I can push that frontier back
Or, perhaps, just step over it
    Unawares.

Beyond This Self

Beyond this self, pain does not exist.
It's closed up in the walls of my flesh,
Like a magnet that has pulled it in from the world.
You might say I've privatised the pain
And now, all around me, there's a luminous void
Like an impenetrable aura that isolates the tumour
About which I know only that it's me.

But then, I also know so little about myself.

Eardrum

That borderline
Is a delicate skin
Stretched between two worlds
Like an eardrum
That can resonate
With the weakest throb,
With the slightest flutter,
That can transmit in vain,
From one side to another
The nothing
That can not become a syllable.

Stele

The symbol of raised palms
Above the gravestone of a child in the times of Augustus
Is a cry of protest against
An unnatural event,
Not a rejection of death in itself,
But only of this particular
Infringement of death's contract with life.
The symbol of raised palms, without arms
With the fingers spread out
As though to ward off something,
That something that cannot be detained by empty hands:
Terror and condemnation living still
Above the gravestone of a dead child
Two thousand years ago.

Wonder

It comes in with a swagger.
It leaves with a shrug.
That timeless time
When wonder flashes into a mind.
Wonder – like a beach ball lost in the sea
That the waves keep bringing back
To the shore,
Only to take it away again –
Without allowing us
One brief respite of meaning.

Recognitions

I'm convinced that I've been here before,
In this body,
In this place,
In this country.
This wonder doesn't stop me
From recognising
What I saw in another time
Or from forgetting that it amazed me then.

Seeds of Stone

If, as St Augustine says,
Evil is nothing more than the absence of Good
And death is the absence of life,
Then in this waste land
We are both evil
And dead,
But we don't know it yet
Because we don't know what
Good is
Or what it is to be alive,
Just as the seeds of stone in the sand
Don't know what it is to germinate.

This Wait

The light is almost green in the air.
Then it goes dark when it turns into sky,
Into glistening roots
And leaves made longer by drops of rain –
This wait
That holds no doubt
Is like the space between a lightning flash
And thunder.
A violent foreboding with no name
Through which startled swallows
Trace uneasy gyres.

Group Portrait

What do they have left?
Dull haloes
Or worse
Trembling skulls,
Voices muffled by time
And the feelings that come back
Remembering long-lost Spains
The fear of losing even their memories,
The uselessness
Of having been defeated by time:
Their hands are withered by arthrosis
But their faith can move even Mount Olympus.

Game

For years now I've thought that
The great misfortune of men
Is that there are too many on the earth.
Although I like to play with children,
Enjoying that ambiguous pleasure,
Almost perverse,
That those who take care of a
Lion or a tiger cub must feel,
As though it were a kitten,
Forgetting that the moment will come when
The play will have to end,
A moment constantly put off
As in a game of Russian roulette.

I play with children who will grow into adults
Always trying to put off that moment
When they'll gleefully tear me apart,
Like adults,
More and more adults,
Always more,
Too many,
While I stay here alone in my childhood.

The Hidden Light

Something catches fire in the hearts of the leaves
And they don't understand what it is,
This change that's happening within.
They sense a light
That they didn't know they bore,
Like Virgins, frightened by the Child,
Like candles, afraid of the flame
That ignites on its own.

Maybe I should try to help them,
But I can't.
That would mean assenting,
Acknowledging
The light I also hide within,
But I put off that painful dawn
From the other side
As though I accepted
That everything has now begun.

Stair Steps

Jericho, Sumer,
Ur, Uruk, Ugarit,
Babylon, Tyre, Sidon,
Memphis, Thebes, Knossos,
Athens, Carthage, Rome,
Byzantium, Constantinople, Istanbul,
Waves of rubble,
Stair steps
To the doorway
(That doesn't, in fact, exist)
Of eternity.

Deflowering

Butterflies and bees –
They follow their own laws.
Lubricious, they hide among the stamens,
While the petals tremble with
Excitement, unable to control their indignation.
Butterflies and bees –
The ambivalent lovers of flowers
That repay them with honey
And with this deflowering –
The departure of pollen
Towards
Their salvation from death.

Pigeons

Hundreds of pigeons, maybe even thousands,
Sitting in obedient pairs
On the sloping roof of the church,
A pigeon to every tile,
Side by side
In evident consent,
Arranged with meticulous care
To transmit or receive
Some message
That you and I are unable to decipher.
We look at them uneasily:
Too many
Clones of the Holy Ghost...

On the Surface of the Universe

I understand so little of the world:
Words surround me
In mists and clouds.
Every now and then some star
With its ruffled edges
Almost introduces a gleam of meaning.
Everything is too far away,
Or else too close,
The lenses are always just out of focus,
Forms with no figure,
No taste, no smell,
Only these fingers, lost
On the rugged surface
Of the universe.

Above the River

In icons hung centuries ago
Above the river
Death is dressed
In the latest cut of clothes
(The latest cut of clothes
When the bridge was built
And the icon was painted).
Timeless Death
Submitted itself to such
Passing fancies.
This tells us that it had a sense of humour,
That it liked to have fun.
It amused itself by dressing up
In the changing fashions
Of the day.
Or maybe it was only the painter
Who amused himself
By painting
His own self-portrait
Above that river
That flows
Towards this future in disguise…

Prayer

God of the dragonflies, of nocturnal moths,
Of larks and owls,
God of earthworms and scorpions,
Of kitchen cockroaches,
God that has taught each one something different
And who knows beforehand what will happen to them all,
I'd like to know what you felt
When you settled
On the sizes
Of their poisons, colours and perfumes,
When you placed a song in one beak
And a cackle in another,
Murder in one soul and ecstasy in another,
I'd give anything to know
If you felt remorse
For making some of them victims and
Others hangmen,
Equally guilty before them all
Because all of them were born with a *fait accompli*.
God of guilt, for having decided on your own
The ratio of evil and good,
The scales trembling always in a delicate balance
Above the wounded body
Of your son, who
Does not resemble you at all.

Seraphim

Three pairs of swans' wings:
One pair to fly,
One to protect your eyes
From the light
And the last one, crossed
Above your sex, which, in reality, doesn't exist,
Just as your eyes don't exist,
Or your ears, or your lips,
Only your place – marked out
As in drawings made by children –
With a name that means
'The one that burns'
(Like the stars that burn in your care:
No ashes,
No smoke,
No sense,
Hundreds of millions).

Multiplication Table

One, two, three
Do whatever you see.
Two, three, four
Life's a stage – nothing more.
Three, four, five
Leap – and feel alive.
Four, five, six
Everything – a mix.
Five, six, seven
Night comes – almost even.
Six, seven, eight
Sleep – and dream your fate.
Seven, eight, nine
Dewdrop falls – so fine.
Eight, nine, ten
Dew dissolves – and you.
The end.

Loneliness

I watch them and their loneliness
Amazes me.
How guilty they are
For being so alone.
I watch them from a distance
And I wonder –
How much loneliness
Can one person stand
Before just dying of loneliness?
And then?

The Slope

How great that I'm not young any more!
I catch myself saying it
Those very few times when
I remember
I'm not young any more.
There are times when it feels like
I'm slipping on a banana peel
Left on a sidewalk covered in the mud of the future
And I desperately want to hold myself back,
Because nothing makes any sense any more
If I can't accept that the street
Is going downhill and
The slope is getting more and more dangerous.

Stairway

I never managed to ascend
From the mysteries of the blood
To the summit of ecstasy.
It was hard climbing up,
I slipped, I fell back again
I tried to figure out
Whether, maybe, I hadn't already got there
Unawares.
I even humiliated myself
By thinking somehow that I was there
And imagining that I felt
What I believed
I was supposed to feel.

Forgive me for this
Inverted mirror image
But on earth as in heaven
Things look alike.
I try to reach you, come close,
Let your aura absorb me,
I imagine that I've touched you –
And I fall into ecstasy
Like birds falling from the sky.
I can't do it.
I never know
If the path goes on
Or if this is all there is.

Forgive me if, powerless,
Full of anger,
I pretend to see you,

I lie to myself,
Making you up
Instead of finding you.
Forgive me for the desecration
Of climbing up this stairway.
Punish me,
Remove it from under my feet
So that I can hang suspended
In a madness
That leaves no room for doubt.

Sweet Confusion

I wear your clothes.
My body fills them.
I'm amazed at how well they fit me,
As though you had come back –
A sweet confusion
Meant to hide
The seed that has passed from one century to another.
I wear your clothes in these streets where you believed.
Make me believe, too.
Let your light glow through me
And the clothes move on their own,
Revealing through the seams
The shining of that seed
That has passed from one century to another.

He

When I say He
I always think about time,
About him with that unspeakable name,
(May the church bells take him)
Who fills us
As though we were bottomless forms,
That he leaves – once he decides
To leave us –
As though we were sad, broken balloons,
The air all whistling out,
And disappearing into nothingness,
Which is to say, into himself…

At the Cello

Like a curtain
Swollen by a breeze born
From the nervous
Wrinkles on that brow,
With no intention or purpose,
Simply there.
Locks of hair conceal and reveal,
Her eyes hidden carefully behind the lids.
Locks of white
Hair, not grey,
That move like smoke or a mist
To cover her age –
Only the agitation
Of her cheek, submerged in mystery,
As though it were a pond
That her forehead churns with its rhythm
Into ripples and waves –
While the locks of hair, like smoke,
Sink,
And are still.

Between Him and Me

Lord, how much life can reside in a tree?
I don't even know his name, but then
I write down my poems every day
On pieces of paper made from his skin.

He has witnessed my winter tears
And I have enjoyed his blossoms when it's warm
Even though my window, looking to the sky,
Doesn't reach as far as his outstretched arms.

When I'm in pain, he
Sings my tribulations.
Even then, between us
There's a silence so enormous
That it takes in everything
From madness to desperation:
Blasphemy, the miracle above,
Prayer and a cry of love.

Sometimes, after ages of this silence between
Us, a single leaf falls down. And then,
Without knowing why, or what the cost,
A grateful universe learns by heart
What it's lost.

A Transparent Being

I've never understood him,
Never could define him:
A transparent being
Or only a breeze
That you don't even feel
Although it brushes your skin.

Only after years or decades
Have passed, you begin to find
His traces
Printed
Deeply on your flesh,
Like the marks of a claw.
The only thing I know about him
Is that he rushes to get
To the place
Where he ceases to exist.

Every 7 Years

If every seven years, as they say,
Nothing in me is the same,
Why should I be surprised to be a stranger?
Alienation is natural.
Everything new
Forgets me and erases me
Just as the sea erases footprints in the sand.

Hollow Walls

We are here
Between hollow walls.
Every night
We drink milk
From our neighbours' cow
Milked by cracked and swollen hands
Like dried-out branches.
We're here
Among ancient plum trees,
Too weak now to give fruit,
And the women are too old to give birth to peasants.
We're here
And we feel good, as though at home
In this world
From which we learn to die.

The Wound

Somebody wrapped barbed wire
Around the cherry tree
And wounded him deeply, pitilessly.
They didn't know a cherry tree could be hurt
(I believe it was Socrates who said that men can be evil
Through their ignorance),
And he started to bleed, a lot, a brown
Viscous liquid, like amber,
Like the blood of a wounded animal instead of a tree.
In the middle of summer his leaves have gone pale
As though so much pain had changed his face.
When you found the barbed wire
You said, 'Our cherry tree is dying,' as though he
Were a member of the family.
And you started, slowly, to pull it out,
Carefully, so he wouldn't feel the pain,
Watching him, from time to time, to see
If the operation was hurting him.
'Do you think he will live?' you asked me at last.
'Of course I do,' I answered,
Knowing that the cherry tree was listening.

Seed of Darkness

The shining body
Shivers with every breath of air
And pours out light
Born every moment
From a seed of darkness
Around the wick, about to disappear,
Only to come back to life
Again, to survive
In the midst of the shining
That makes it possible –
This almost sensual dance
At the top of the candle
About to go out
Like faith
Put to the test, uncertain, growing larger, content,
Then bending over, flickering, desperate,
Reduced to a seed of darkness
From which it will burn again.

Requiem

1

'Who is that behind you?' you asked me.
I didn't dare to turn my head.
I only murmured, 'No one.'
'But,' you said, 'I see him
And I want to know who it is.'
Without turning round
I whispered: 'It's Nobody.'

2

Your voice and the sound of the rain
Tied me in
Like a strait jacket.
There was no escape.
Rhythmically, always with the beat
Of the sound of the rain and your voice
You begged: 'Oh Lord, let this end.
Please, let it end.'
You
Lord, who embraces me in compassion
Like a strait jacket
Without deciding
To listen
Or to ignore her prayer.

3

How does it feel
When something pushes you from behind,
Somebody or something,
And you aren't able to resist
And you don't know where to go

While it pushes you faster and faster –
Sometimes you can't even
Take one step
And you slip,
Or you slide
For a space,
But you can't be sure that
You can fly,
When your only possibility
At the sudden end of the path
Is flight…

4

I said to you
'A poet, whom I don't think you've read,
Believed that
In the beyond
There is also death
And its outcome is to be born on the earth.'
And, for a moment, you forgot your pain,
You smiled at me,
Sad,
As though it were a joke,
And I went on, to make you laugh:
'If you don't feel at home there,
Remember Novalis.
And, above all, don't forget
To tie a knot in your handkerchief
To let me know
When you're coming back.'

5

Bringer of good news,
His shadow resting
On the wall

At the head of your bed:
He was waiting,
Had probably already told it
And expected you to be glad
But you didn't hear
And you hadn't seen him
And you kept on suffering
While he,
With his wings all tensed
Stared and stared
To see if you were breathing or not.

6

You were so lovely,
Almost translucent –
Still a body, but a body
That contained a light that
Drew your shape on the pillow,
A silver-tinted shadow –
Even then, a shadow
You began to belong
To another world, to another state of being
Even then,
Even before.

25 September 2005
9-9:30 am

7

If time is the life of the soul
As Plotinus said,
Then I have less soul now
Than I had ten years ago
And you have almost none.
But it's not that way.
Nothing is lost:

Time builds up in the soul
Like an hourglass, with falling grains of sand,
Each one born from the thoughts, the sparks
That you
Constantly weave,
An hourglass that,
If you want to,
You only have
To turn over.

8

I knew that you would see us from above
As though you had been buried in heaven
Before being buried in the grave,
Or, as though everything were a reflection,
On earth
As it is in heaven,
I remembered
That strict look
You used to have
– no use hiding anything from you –
And, like before,
I was afraid and
I wanted to obey you
But I no longer knew what it meant
To be obedient.

9

The fact that I can't see you,
That now we can't meet any more,
That I go to
Pick up the phone we used to talk on
And stop my hand in midair –
None of that means that you aren't here.

Maybe you're just late
Or very deep
Like the lowest note of an organ, that
No one can hear.

10

Your voice speaks out of every clod of earth.
I hear it in my sleep.
That same voice that called to me in my dreams
When I was a child
And I woke up in tears
And you were there to soothe me:
'Don't cry, don't cry…'
'I dreamed that you were dead
And that you called to me from there,' I said.
'Don't cry, don't cry'
You tell me
'There is here.'

11

Do not let me
Fall into the future
And unweave myself in time to come
Like some winged animal
Buried on foreign horizons
In the grave of the sky.
Be my anchor
In the clay.
Weigh me down with the grass
Here, in the present
That has already passed away.
Be my anchor
And ask…

12

'Write,' you told me.
And I took pencil and paper
Thinking you wanted to dictate something to me.
'Write,' you repeated.
But you were as silent as an icon.
So I have begun to write
Your silence.
Your silence that everything flows from,
Like blood flows from a wound.

Black Cherries

Cherry trees beaten by a pitiless wind –
Their branches clash and scrape
And suddenly wrap together
Embracing each other with a hate in
Spite of which they manage to bring forth
Small, black spheres whose taste is both
Bitter and sweet.

This sweet and bitter fruit
Leaves the marks of its ink
On my lips and my fingers.
Are they trying to write on me
That ancient, secret proportion,
The golden mean between extremes?

The wind erases from this tainted skin
The indecipherable stains
Of good and evil,
Of the sweet and the bitter.

Mysteries

When I stare at the leaves of the oak tree
Afflicted by a wind that only they can feel,
The mystery of Dodona seems more comprehensible
And I find myself imagining Zeus in exile.
It's odd that men never wonder
Where the gods live when they stop being gods,
Immortals obliged to live out their eternity
Deprived of power. Humiliated,
They become the invisible audience of our
World that does not even recognise its mysteries.

Sometimes, nevertheless, I feel them come close:
Apollo appears in my dreams, opens the door,
I hear his footsteps on the kitchen floor,
He goes through my papers, touches the keyboard,
And then he stops for a while to look at the crucifix –
Maybe then he understands
How one set of mysteries has taken the place of another.

Island

I'd like to be an island
In the dreams of those who want to be alone,
Or one that the shipwrecked see in their hallucinations,
An island rhythmically embraced by the waves
That pull away and come back forever.

A handful of trees, some beaches, a cliff –
Brief definition of loneliness
For all of those people
Who cannot imagine that
An island is the summit of a mountain
On whose slopes live thousands of beings
In the depths of the sea.

Continual Loss

Losing isn't hard,
It can even be a pleasure in itself,
Embarrassing due to the inexplicable joy
It contains –
A way to find out you can live
Without whatever you've lost.

And, even if you've lost someone you love
The pain includes a tiny
Iota of freedom,
So small that it could be a seed
From which, despite the tears,
Something else can be born.

Losing isn't hard,
In fact, ascension is nothing more
Than a continual loss,
The burden of those objects and beings that you've left behind
Helps you to rise,
Impels you towards the chaos
Where loneliness
Becomes the raw material
For palaces of ancient dreams
Where no one lives any more.

Parallels

No hope of waking up.
We're closed in our own dream
Like a capsule, hermetically sealed,
Where each one dreams a different dream
And never thinks it might not be reality.

Sleeping soldiers, armed to the teeth,
Stumble ahead with helmets, mess kits, blankets, supplies,
Tools they use – without waking up – to kill
Other soldiers submerged in a parallel dream.
While, from their own nightmare,
Cataleptic historians
Write chronicles
Of it all,
And poets dream that they wake up and discover
That reality is somewhere else.

Restorations

What narrow boundaries I'm able to take in with
My heart and my eyes!
I travel in vain. No matter how far I go,
I'm only moved by
The familiar, what I recall somehow
From my childhood, or much earlier,
From a previous life
I know nothing about, but try to put together
Like a puzzle
With the scattered fragments I can recognise.
The terrain I assemble this way –
Out of gestures suspended in the middle of the air
That become immortal
Has such narrow and happy borders.
At the end of the day,
Immortality is nothing more than the stubbornness
Of remembering
Lives that were powerful enough
To come to life again.

Lament

One long cry that doesn't even
Stop to breathe,
To lick away the salt left by tears on the lips,
A cry like the siren of an ambulance
Speeding through the streets with a suffering
That hasn't yet become a cadaver,
A cry like some hysterical horn
In a traffic jam, trying to squeeze through,
A cry that drowns out the voices of the city,
That penetrates walls, roof tiles,
Double-glazed windows, eiderdowns covering heads,
Earplugs,
And reaches into the ultimate cell of the brain,
A cry from the hoarser and hoarser throat of an angel
Who cannot find its way back home.

Country of Unease

This is the country of unease,
Always about to change its mind
Any second now
Without, however, giving up hope of
Some indefinite possibility.
This is my native land,
Between these walls
The handful of metres between
And not even all of them –
Alone at the desk with paper and pencils
Ready to move on their own and begin to write,
Skeletons brought suddenly to life by ancient feathers
Unused for ages, the glue dried out –
They scribble in a frenzy on the paper
And leave no trace…
This is the country of unease:
Will I manage some day
To decipher these traces that no one can see
But that I know are there, and waiting
For me to write them out
In my native land: A4?

POETRY BETWEEN SILENCE AND SIN

THE FIRST TIME IN MY LIFE I saw a printed poem I was only five or six years old. I hardly even knew how to read when I was given a book of children's verse. Even today I remember how surprised I was – before I began to decipher the poems letter by letter – to see how few words it contained. Compared with my father's voluminous tomes, whose pages were replete with letters, *my* book seemed so poor; every page had only a handful of shortened lines, leaving more than ample room for colourful illustrations in those untroubled empty spaces. When I asked why my book had such a paucity of words, the answer was brief and simple: 'That's the way poetry is.'

This surprising discovery, in fact, was the source of my first attempts at writing verse. I was in primary school – maybe the second grade – and the teacher told us to write a story about our summer holidays. She said that when we had written at least two pages, we could go out to recess. I remembered those blank spaces in my little poetry book and asked her how many pages of verses we should write. I thought she'd answer 'a lot'. But to my surprise, she said that if I could write verses, I would only have to write one page. That was how I started to understand the strange relationship between poetry and words. With the passing of time, that relationship has proved to be inversely proportional; it has led me finally to realise that, in a world where so much is written and said, the ultimate purpose of a poem should be to re-establish silence.

In the beginning was the epic: an immense river of words, moulded with rhythm and rhyme, that contained absolutely everything. There wasn't the slightest room for doubt; everything was fully expressed, from the anger of Achilles to the metamorphosis of Narcissus to *The Legend of the Centuries*.[1] What we think of as poetry today only existed

---

1. Victor Hugo's epic work (1859) that synthesized the history of the world.

in the pauses for breath between hexameters, or the caesuras of alexandrines or in the empty spaces between words. Philosophical poetry does not consist in pronouncing wise phrases, but in expressing the silence that embraces words.

Whoever realised this became the first great modern poet. Over the course of time, the counting of metres has turned out to be laughable, one step forward and who knows how many back. Romanticism has churned out reams of versified stories in the manner of Villon's *Ballad of the Ladies of Yesteryear*. Poetry is not a series of events, but a sequence of visions. It's not a matter of banal abbreviation or simple concentration; but of essence and symbol. And when I say 'symbol', I do not mean the word or trope, or the movement called 'Symbolism'; I am thinking of a mathematical symbol. In an infinitely longer time, poetry – like mathematics – has moved from things to the symbol, from the numbering of objects to the naked cypher itself. Poetry has turned its back on words in the same way that the plastic arts have turned their backs on form, and music on melody. This is, in a sense, a rejection of the artist's proper means of expression, a process that recalls the reaction of the sculptor who throws away his chisel when he realises that he can give life to the marble statue with his breath. This rejection signals the degree of an artist's self-confidence.

With the discovery of the concept of suggestion, the evocative power of the word came to be both the definition of poetry and its unit of measure. Now neither what is said nor how it is said is as important as what is suggested through the word. The determining factor is only the relation between what is pronounced and what is understood. And the higher the ratio of inference to speech, the closer the verses come to poetry. The eloquence of poetry is no longer measured by a particular combination of words, but by the silences between them. The ideal is to express the least possible in order to suggest much more. And from this point, my thinking jumps involuntarily ahead: if saying little in order to suggest a lot supposed an artistic advance, then saying even less to suggest more is another step forward, and not saying anything in order to suggest everything is the culmination of the process. Where nothing is said, all can be suggested. Mallarmé was the first to prefer silence to poetry. This may seem like madness, but it's logical, since silence contains all poetry in the same way that the colour white contains all the other colours.

Having put forth this definition of modern poetry – that accounts more easily for Novalis than for Aragon – I cannot help but ask myself who would be able to distinguish silence from serenity. Who would be able to distinguish that moment when the song ascends from one soul to another, from brow to brow, while the wells of communication remain unseen, and the murmur of the moment unheard, that moment when, face to face and with empty eyes, we will not have anything to say?

How can we distinguish the poetry of the future from what a philosopher has called 'death by an infinity of information'? What delicate device will have to be invented to detect and differentiate silence from serenity?

Of course, there is no answer to this question. In artistic communication, all five – or maybe more? – of the senses participate in the relationship between the creating mind and the receiving mind. Thus, the imperfection of the senses accounts for the imperfection of art, since art can neither exist exclusively through the senses nor beyond them. But if art is the yearning for perfection, and perfection, like all absolute values, only exists somewhere beyond the limits of the real, then art is a yearning for non-existence, for non-being, and the work of art itself is that tenuous and imprecise boundary between existence and non-existence. Poetry then is not so much a form of survival as a form of death, a mode of endless dying, like the ticking of a clock, a dying that can never be finished. Eternity is nothing more than a death without end. Only the imperfect can exist. Poetry tends towards perfection, yet that poetry that reaches perfection disappears. In this sense, the great work of art is not a matter of form, but of the absence of form. As soon as the poet transcribes his faith into tropes, he implicitly accepts the degradation of that faith through multiplication, fragmentation or an incomplete or erroneous comprehension resulting from its expression. The greatest and truest poetry is that which has not yet been formulated. The ineffable, that cannot be named, hovers and bewitches, behind every line. With every line he writes, the poet betrays his latent perfection. Maybe the great poet should never write a single line. Those poets who die young come closest to this absurd ideal. I say *absurd* because the poet can die, but not the poetry: although we have been used for centuries to seeing ships float on the surface of the sea, we do not believe that a submarine perishes when it sinks into the depths and its antennas disappear from sight.

But no poet, no matter how great – or maybe because of his greatness – will ever renounce his final words. He will always be torn between the desire to let his song flow from him softly and silently, almost senselessly, as the blood flows through the veins, and the temptation to make himself understood by a multitude, a group, one person. To give up words, although desired with exasperation by the great poet, would be a superhuman act, a step too far. Century after century, hour after hour, we witness the descent of poetry into the depths of silence, or only into the depths of language; we witness how words withdraw into themselves – as a snail, disappointed by what it discovers, retracts its antennae – in a process that has no end, like time. There is no form beyond the imperfection of the senses, and perfection is a question of form. The movement arising from this contradiction will never cease, and the definition of poetry is rooted precisely in this *perpetuum mobile.*

To what extent can the poet – I myself – resist this logical sequence of judgements and the conclusions it has generated? The first reaction, psychological in nature, is a certain fear of literature (and poetry is always to be found on the farther rather than the nearer side of literature). This fear of the ordering of language, of the artifice of words terrifies me and, at times, leaves me completely incapable of expression. After the spontaneous appearance of the first couple of lines, a kind of shy and obstinate pride keeps me from intentionally completing something that began without my willing it. I believe this must be Montale's famous '*non sapere inventare nulla*'.[2] I, too, am incapable of inventing anything. I can only transcribe what I experience. I am not a writer, only a poet. At certain moments of grace, to a greater degree than the rest of the time, I have always had the strange and paradoxically flattering feeling that it isn't I who writes, but some other person who expresses through me things that I hadn't even imagined a few moments before writing them.

Maybe I should be offended by this total dependence on forces that I cannot even minimally influence, but I feel happy and as proud as a lady in waiting that the king has chosen to bear his child. This is an odd combination of humility and pride that can only result in a special form of liberation. I was convinced until recently that I write because someone inside of me dictates, word for word, something that I have to hurriedly write down, and that I only have to create the necessary conditions for this inner voice to speak, and not stop speaking. And although it would be an exaggeration to claim that I myself am that voice, a deep sense of kinship, a veritable blood relationship, exists between my pages and me. Now it seems that this someone has installed himself outside of me and, taciturn and uncommunicative, will not bother to clarify anything, but instead, simply takes my hand and moves it across the paper.

And so, as though it were a conversation in a language that I don't know well – my own variation on a notion of T.S. Eliot – I am surprised to find myself saying something different from what I thought because, since I can't come up with the exact words I need, I have to use others with a slightly different meaning. When I write I am unable to follow a precise plan – which, on the other hand, I never try to do – because other vowels, different from the ones I was looking for, steal their way into my phrase and generate meanings that I hadn't intended. Therefore, where poetry is concerned, I have enough common sense to avoid specific aims. I am a poet; I cannot allow myself to become a versifier. But calling myself a poet makes me feel uneasy, not just because that claim could be immodest, but

---

2. I don't know how to invent anything.

because it is a somewhat indecent confession. I have never been able to say 'we poets' without embarrassment, just as I have never been able to say 'we women' without blushing. It is as though I were alluding to secret, irrational concepts that shouldn't be named out loud.

Poetry has given me a sense of the *other* in the world that surrounds us, that other that I would only call *no one* during moments of exhaustion. And although I'm aware that it's not I who have the power of decision over my pages, a condition I am actually proud of, I am committed to write, determined not only to express myself, but also to exist in order to be expressed. I am like a woollen fleece that exists only if someone spins it.

It follows, then, that the relationship between poetry and literature is complex and contradictory. Poetry is not in the slightest, as we were taught in grade school, just another literary genre, a simple fragment of literature. While the raw material of literature is words, the mystery of poetry is composed of those silences whose borders words can only mark out and give value to. This is why meanings constantly slip and slide in a mysterious polyvalence that creates a halo around words, like the haloes crowning the heads of the saints. The mystery is never nebulous. It begins not here but on the other side of clarity. The strangest and most difficult poems are not those in which we cannot understand a thing, but those that can never be completely understood. There are, in fact, poets who refuse to communicate, and others who remain enigmatic when they do communicate, while the mystery underlies even the illusory certainty of those who believe that they have understood everything.

For me, poetry is a logical advance from one word to the next, from one stone to the next, on solid ground, up to the point where meaning suddenly and unexpectedly opens out above the void, and you stop and hold your breath. That moment is everything, that irruption of the abyss, that sudden gasp of breath before the boundary; that halt is more revealing than the pathway that takes us over the precipice. Rather than the miraculous, I have always preferred those questions that have no reply from which the miraculous ultimately arises. A poem seduces me to the degree in which its logic conserves the footprints of the logic of others, those mysterious signs laden with indecipherable meanings, like some incomprehensible memories from a previous life that – we can't deny it now – one time existed. I have always dreamed of a text with a number of distinct, independent and perfectly intelligible levels, like the walls of some medieval monasteries covered with landscapes in which, from certain angles, the figures of the saints can be discerned. The important thing in poetry is not the new or the unheard-of, but something that we know from another life. Poetry should not aim to transmit knowledge, or cognition, but a feeling of re-cognition.

I think I should have begun by confessing that I have never cultivated the unseen, the unsaid, the original or the new in search of admiration or fame. I have always believed that poetry should illuminate rather than dazzle. That emblematic line of Baudelaire's, '*Au fond de l'inconnu, pour trouver le Nouveau*'[3] has always seemed alien and incomprehensible to me because the arrogant desire to search for and find the New, which is to say, success, belongs to a lower and more mundane territory than that of poetry. Related more with the desire to cause sensation than to be, the pursuit of originality seems to me frivolous and prone to break the link between form and content for the sake of the unusual. The architects of the Gothic cathedrals did not try to avoid repeating the art of their predecessors, on the contrary, they strove not to differentiate themselves from each other. Though it may seem paradoxical, the great poets resemble each other, while only the weaker ones strive to be original. The sublime has little diversity. Those who achieve it are similar. In their best and highest lines, Shakespeare and Novalis are similar. The ineffable has no categories. Only the mediocre are different, original and diverse. It isn't hard to be new; it is hard to be timeless. Poetry and pride are incompatible. Though it isn't always evident, there is a significant

---

3. 'To the depths of the abyss to find the New.'

difference between the poet and the poseur, between the one who writes and the one who only wants to be crowned with laurels.

I gave up, long ago, the illusion that I could control my poetry through reason and renounced the ambition to do so. There was a time when the gap between my conscious intelligence and my art seemed to be an injustice I had to rebel against. Only when I understood that poetry is a function of silence, more akin to stillness and shadows than to inner turmoil and blinding light, only then did I understand why the gods so often chose to send clumsy and dull-witted beings to the earth. Now I have come to fear the pride of wanting to understand everything and of wanting to completely eliminate anything that cannot be comprehended through the intellect. At times, I even think that poetry means the denial of the intellect.

But if intellectual ability and a rational approach can be opposed to the essence of poetry, can the same be said of aesthetic structures, the norms of beauty, tropes and embellishments? There are very few points where poetry and literary doctrines intersect, and theories concerning poetry and poetics usually come from authors who find it easier to talk about poetry than to create it. Giordano Bruno intuited as much when he complained about those 'who make rules for poetry', rules that would be completely ignored by the true poets. Those fixed forms of elaborate versification that have held sway with such doctrinaire authority for whole centuries – '*toute est prose rimée*' said Rimbaud – frighten me with their ability to cover the empty void with beautiful upholstery, with their treachery of creating sophisticated and corseted uniforms that can equally clothe either poetry or nothingness. There are many poems that remind me of those medieval costumes conserved in museums, costumes so heavily adorned that they stand up proudly on their own, without the need to clothe a living body.

I know that all true poetry is strong enough to overcome the obstacles of its own embellishments. I dream of a poetry so simple, clean and transparent that it doesn't even seem to be there, a poetry whose words come together in response to mysterious orders rather than inflexible laws. I dream of a melody of sounds, flowing to rhythms set by music unhampered by the forced calculation of metrics. I fear mechanical rhyme, that falls like an implacable blade at the end of every line; I am enchanted by the kind of irregular rhymes that appear unexpectedly in the distance and bring new life to some forgotten meaning, like a long-lost love. Those rhymes that make me feel that I'm joining words that knew each other in another life excite me; while obvious, erudite and offensive rhymes frighten me like the shards of a mirror that, instead of reflecting a face, slyly dazzle us with the sun in our eyes. Because nothing frightens me more than that talent that can be discerned at first sight and that rhetoric that cannot be intuited from the beginning.

But we could endlessly analyse the aversion that every true poet feels for literature, an aversion that constitutes the definition of the contradictory nature of poetic creation, which always resides somewhere between the artistic gesture and the mystical one. 'We are more closely connected to the invisible than the visible,' said Novalis, giving us a simple description of the unstable and uncertain balance between beauty and truth. Is this a sin? Is this perhaps the original sin, that strongly, though reluctantly, links the magic of matter with our need to go beyond it? And, in a similar sense, is the poet to be held guilty for this double need to be both understood and not understood by others? Especially since for many decades now the drama of the poet has not been the indifference of society, but the zeal with which society embraces, manipulates and elevates him into a symbol. Having to choose between the sin of the spoken word and that of silent suggestion, between the acceptance and the rejection of material – and therefore limited – expression, poetry has to take a side with every line put down. Poetry itself postpones that dramatic choice until the very moment when its birth can no longer be avoided. The implacable nature of poetry is its only, painful reason to be. And pain is always a certainty in such uncertain territory.

I cannot end these notes without repenting of having tried to talk about things that cannot really be expressed. Referring to the supreme reality, and therefore also to poetry, Lao Tze says, 'He who knows, does not speak; he who speaks, does not know.' But who can say more about poetry than poetry itself? No one asks a question without at least a sense of the reply. In spite of this, however, I have no doubt that to a common horse the wings of Pegasus would only seem to prove that he was not fit to run.

ANA BLANDIANA

THE TRANSLATORS

Paul Scott Derrick is a Senior Lecturer in American literature at the University of Valencia. His main field of interest encompasses Romanticism and American Transcendentalism and their influences on subsequent artistic and intellectual manifestations of the 20th and 21st centuries. His critical works include *Thinking for a Change: Gravity's Rainbow and Symptoms of the Paradigm Shift in Occidental Culture* (1994) and *We stand before the secret of the world: Traces along the Pathway of American Transcendentalism* (2003). He has edited and co-translated into Spanish a number of critical editions of works by Ralph Waldo Emerson, Emily Dickinson (Spanish and Catalan), Henry Adams and Sarah Orne Jewett. He is co-editor, with Viorica Patea, of *Modernism Revisited: Transgressing Boundaries and Strategies of Renewal in American Poetry* (Rodopi, 2007) and is, with Norman Jope and Catherine E. Byfield, co-editor of *The Salt Companion to Richard Berengarten* (Salt, 2011). With Miguel Teruel, he has published a translation of Richard Berengarten's *Black Light* into Spanish (Luz Negra, JPM Ediciones, 2012); and with Viorica Patea, a translation into English of Ana Blandiana's *My Native Land A4* (Bloodaxe Books, 2014). He is currently coordinating a series of critical studies and Spanish translations of Emily Dickinson's fascicles.

Viorica Patea is Associate Professor of American Literature at the University of Salamanca, where she teaches American and English literature. Her published books include *Entre el mito y la realidad: Aproximación a la obra poética de Sylvia Plath* (Ediciones Universidad de Salamanca 1989), a study on Whitman, *La apología de Whitman a favor de la épica de la modernidad* (Ediciones Universidad de León, 1999) and *T.S. Eliot's The Waste Land* (Cátedra: 2005). She has edited various collections of essays, such as *Critical Essays on the Myth of the American Adam* (Ediciones Universidad de Salamanca, 2001) and, together with Paul Scott Derrick, *Modernism Revisited: Transgressing Boundaries and Strategies of Renewal in American Poetry* (Rodopi 2007).

Her most recent publication is a collection of essays, *Short Story Theories: A Twenty-First-Century Perspective* (Rodopi 2012), which received the Javier Coy Research Award for the best edited book (2013) from the Spanish Association of American Studies. Her research interests include comparative studies in witness literature of East European countries. In collaboration with Fernando Sánchez Miret, she has translated from Romanian into Spanish the annotated edition of *El diario de la felicidad* by Nicolae Steinhardt (Sígueme 2007) and *Proyectos de Pasado* and *Las Cuatro estaciones* by Ana Blandiana (Periférica 2008, 2011). She is also co-translator, with Paul Scott Derrick, of Ana Blandiana's *My Native Land A4* (Bloodaxe Books, 2014).